THE CATHOLIC SACRAMENT OF RECONCILIATION: LIVING LIFE TO THE FULLEST

A Catholic Philosopher`s Reflection

Rev Fr Joachim Ireruke Ukutsemuya, Ph.D

Amazon (KDP)

Cover design by: Self from KDP Gallery

This reflection titled: The Catholic Sacrament of Reconciliation: Living life to the Fullest, A Catholic Philosopher`s Reflection is dedicated to two ends. Firstly to the 20th priestly ordination anniversary of my Warri diocesan classmates Rev. Fathers: Charles Epetuku, Mark Ikeke, Jude Sagbodje, Royston Onogagamue and then my humble self. Secondly, this work is dedicated to the memory of the year of Mercy declared by his Holiness Pope Francis emphasizing Mercy as the core of Christianity and charging Christians to be merciful as God is.

CONTENTS

INTRODUCTION

When I was growing up, at the mention of the sacrament of reconciliation, also commonly known as the sacrament of confession, minds of my age mate go to that scenario of the human person having to once a while remember the task of eternal life where you have to periodically cleanse yourself of your sins to enable you receive the holy communion on Sundays and also to be prepared for the call of God that could come at any time.

The penance given by the priest then was never to be forgotten, which ranges from saying a few prayers to doing some works with positive impacts on the lives of people and community.

All of the above was my mentality and that of some of my age mate about the sacrament of reconciliation when we were growing up. However, like the usual experience of the young person about life that is never profound and in need of the full light, our picture of this precious sacrament was far from the truth about it.

This write-up titled: **The Catholic Sacrament of Reconciliation: Living life to the Fullest,** *A Catholic Philosopher`s Reflection,* explores the beautiful theology of God`s creation and redemption of our world through His love, with the human person at the center. The book reveals the essential connection of the sacrament to the work of salvation that Jesus Christ accomplished for our world. As the work of Christ was basically the deliverance of the human person and his/her world from the kingdom of darkness and evil to a kingdom of light and goodness of life, the sacrament of reconciliation is powerfully revealed as a means of recapturing the goodness of life which is always diminished, rubbished and ruined by sin.

Consequently, the sacrament of confession becomes a precious opportunity of reconnection with the beautiful destiny that God has destined for all humans. It is, therefore, much more than enabling us to receive the holy communion on Sundays or to eventually secure heaven when death comes knocking. Indeed, the sacrament of reconciliation installs humans in the glorious life of goodness from the hand of an omnipotent and a benevolent God. It all comes down to the truth that: if you desire the good life, then you need the sacrament of reconciliation which removes the evil life and ensures the good life, the wish of God every day for the human person.

Enjoy your reading!

Very Rev Fr Dr Joachim Ireruke Ukutsemuya

CHAPTER ONE

The Catholic Sacrament
of Reconciliation

The Merriam Webster's College dictionary, tenth edition, in one of its meanings, defines reconciliation as the action of reconciling. In Philosophy, this kind of definition is what is known as a circular definition. This is because in explaining the meaning of a word, the word that is explained is used.

Though the definition of reconciliation above may be circular, it is however, a good place to begin the discussion of the Sacrament of Reconciliation in the Catholic Church.

The same dictionary in explaining the word "reconcile" says it is: to restore to friendship or harmony. It is pertinent to note here that the presupposition in this explanation is that there is a disagreement or separation that now requires bringing together or making to come to harmony.

It is no wonder the Vatican II document under the heading "Degree on the Missionary Activity of the Church" paragraph 3, says:

> *In order to establish peace or communion between sinful human beings and Himself, as well as to fashion them into a fraternal community, God determined to intervene in human history in*

a way both new and definitive. For He sent His son clothed in our flesh, in order that through this Son He might snatch men from the power of darkness and of Satan (Col 1:13; Acts 10:38) and that in this Son He might reconcile the world to Himself (2 Cor.5:19).

From the above document, we can begin to understand the disagreement or separation that is implied in the idea of reconciliation. The disagreement in this context therefore, is the separation of human beings by themselves, through sin, from God.

In an understanding that is in harmony with the discussion here contained, the Catholic Catechism in its glossary defines the Sacrament of Reconciliation as the sacramental celebration in which, through God's mercy and forgiveness, the sinner is reconciled with God and also with the church, Christ's body, which is wounded. And in Article 1422: the Catechism explains that those who approach the Sacrament of Penance obtain pardon from God's mercy for the offense committed against Him and are, at the same time, reconciled with the Church which they have wounded by their sins and which by charity, by example, and by prayer labors for their conversion.

Explaining further, the Catholic Catechism holds that the sacrament of reconciliation is called the Sacrament of Conversion because it makes sacramentally present, Jesus' call to conversion, the first step in returning to the Father from whom one has strayed by sin.

It is known as the Sacrament of Penance because it consecrates the Christian sinner's personal and ecclesial steps of conversion, penance, and satisfaction.

It is referred to as Sacrament of Confession because the sacrament essentially involves the sinner's confession of his or her sins to a priest.

It is identified as the Sacrament of Forgiveness because by the priest's sacramental absolution, God grants the "penitent peace."

It is the Sacrament of Reconciliation because it gives to the sinner the love of God, who reconciles.

In all of the different ways in which the Sacrament of Reconciliation is designated, it is sufficient to understand that it is God's action through the instrumentality of the Church and her representatives by which God brings His beloved creature, the human person, to Himself: He who is the genuine peace of man.

In a manner that maintains the main idea running through the Sacrament of Reconciliation, St. Paul in his letter to the Corinthians says:

> *It is all God's work; He reconciled us to Himself through Christ and He gave us the ministry of reconciliation. I mean God was in Christ reconciling the world to Himself, not holding anyone's fault against them, but entrusting to us the message of reconciliation. (2 Cor. 5:18-19)*

On the part of Pope John Paul II, in his encyclical, "Rich in Mercy." he says:

> *It is God who is rich in mercy. It is He whom Jesus Christ has revealed to us as Father...God, who is rich in mercy, out of the great love with which He loved us, even when we were dead through our trespasses, made us alive together with Christ.*

In all of the above then, reconciliation is the means by which God restores man to the original state that man was made to be in: the state of peace, grace and indeed blessed life of God. God takes the initiative of reconciling man to Himself because, although the human person strayed from God through his doings, God being love and good by nature, does not abandon man to his fate of estrangement from God, a life of frustration, meaninglessness, misery and all unfriendly human situations. God seeks to reconcile man (the human person) to Himself. It is for this reason that the Eucharistic prayer IV says:

> *Even when he (the human person) disobeyed you and lost your friendship, you did not abandon him to the power of death.... Again and again you offered a covenant to man.*

The covenant that is offered to man (the human person) is indeed one that will return the human person to genuine life that God intends for the human person when He created him/her.

CHAPTER TWO

*Implications of the Catholic
Sacrament of Reconciliation*

The sacrament of reconciliation has nothing in connection with the idea of show-off. It is therefore not an opportunity for the human person to show how holy he or she is. This will mean when we go for the sacrament of reconciliation, we are to be yearning for reconciliation with God, the author of life, as non-reconciliation with Him will mean being cut-off from the author and supplier of life and energy for living. This is so because it will follow that a life that is lived outside of being reconciled to God will be a life that is inauthentic in as much as that is not how God intends it when he made the human person. Being inauthentic, it is bound to be in crisis, the life characterized by frustrations, meaninglessness and lack of warmth needed to carry on in life.

If the Sacrament of Reconciliation as explicated above enables us to be linked with the source of our lives, being at home with ourselves, and getting the energy for living, then nothing whatsoever in life must deter or discourage us from going to confessions irrespective of how frequent this might be. This is because there are some Catholics who because they go to confession confessing the same sins all the time, conclude the idea of confession is useless.

They ask for the reasonability of going for confessions when they are not able to overcome their habitual sins.

It should be known that as long as we commit sins, confession is the means of getting back to the proper order of life. As mentioned already, when we live the life that is not reconciled to God, we make available to ourselves another world that is surely unfriendly to the human person. This is not to scare us! It only needs to be emphasized that we are not to be discouraged from availing ourselves for confessions because of the weakness of habitual sins. Our relationship with God is what is involved, and that is what matters! Let us turn to God as often as we commit sins! We are not pleasing human beings! We are simply striving to be united with our creator, in whom we are at home, in whom we are at peace! Avoiding confession, therefore, amounts to depriving ourselves of the peace we desperately need in life.

The sacrament of reconciliation provides us with the opportunity to get all evils out of our bodies. As we read from Gen.1: 26, the human person was made in the image and likeness of God. The image and likeness of God is that of love and goodness. Evil therefore gets us out of our nature which is love and goodness. This situation leads to crisis because our real nature has been perverted by the presence of evil. It is this crisis that Father Oscar Lukefahr states in a different way when he said:

Many psychologists are now saying that when we keep guilt and other negative feelings inside, they cause stress, which is harmful to our emotional and physical health. The same psychologists point out that talking about our guilt with another person has a cleansing effect and helps us gain new insights to face the future. Our sins and our failings seem less overwhelming when we "get them out of our system." (Father Oscar Lukefahr, 1993:92-93)

In essence, it is to be understood that the sacrament of reconciliation makes available God's means for humans to get their sins and failings out of their systems. The moment of sacramental reconciliation becomes a wonderful moment in the lives of humans. It fixes our beings, bodies, and systems back to order. The absence of which leaves our bodies, systems and beings in brokenness, which in other words, is **state of crisis**. No human being wants to remain in a state of crisis!

Besides, the human person is a part of nature. The laws of nature are the laws of God. As long as the human person remains steadfast in the will of God, he or she is in harmony with nature, the greatest peace of the human person. However, when the human person breaks out of the laws of nature, he or she lives in brokenness waiting to be mended or restored to its original state of harmony with the rest of the things of nature through the sacrament of reconciliation. Oh, what peace and bliss the sacrament of reconciliation makes available!

CHAPTER THREE

*The Process of the Catholic
Sacrament of Reconciliation*

For a moment, let's see what happens when a penitent goes for the sacrament of reconciliation. The penitent goes to the priest and says, "Father, bless me for I have sinned." The priest says "May God be on your heart and your lips in order to confess your sins worthily." With all other procedures observed, the penitent begins to confess his or her sins. At the end of the confession, he or she says "Bless me, for these I remember and others I do not remember." The priest then lovingly exhorts the penitent in the manner of a loving father. The priest gives the penitent penance and asks the penitent to say the Act of Contrition which goes essentially thus: "O my God, I am very sorry that I have sinned against you. By the help of your grace, I will not sin again." The priest then gives the absolution in the following words:

> *God, the father of mercies, through the death and resurrection of His son has reconciled the world to Himself and sent the Holy Spirit among us for the forgiveness of sins; through the ministry of the church may God give you pardon and peace, and I absolve you from your sins in the name of the Father, and of the Son, and of the Holy Spirit.*

The penitent responds, *"Amen."*

A critical look at the whole process of the sacrament of reconciliation reveals that it is a whole process intended by God through the church to sufficiently purge the penitent of all evils and guilt that cause crisis in the person in order to leave the person liberated and at peace with himself/herself. Oh, what a great thing the sacrament of reconciliation is!

However, some Catholics, in their love for God go to an extreme! They are so scrupulous when it comes to sin. They get so worried about their sins being forgiven. Sometimes, because they forget to confess a venial sin, that is, a minor sin, they get so disturbed whether they are in good relationship with God. Whatever may be the cause of the scrupulosity, it is important to know that God is good, loving and all knowing. As a result of these attributes of His, God knows our hearts. He knows who we are and what we go through in preparation for confessions. Therefore, after doing all the necessary preparations for the sacrament of reconciliation and we find ourselves to have forgotten some minor sins, especially when we say: **"forgive me for these I remember and others I do not remember,"** let us be assured that God will make things right and grant us his forgiveness and absolution, especially once our sins have been confessed and forgiveness obtained, no matter how serious our sins may be, once forgiven by a priest they are truly forgiven. God remains good and loving; He does not hold the sins of anyone against him/her. He (God) only wants us to repent and live according to His will where there is true life, and where we can get the utmost from life. Let us then concentrate more on the goodness and love nature of God, not to enable us to do the wrong but to marvel us to do the right thing.

CHAPTER FOUR

*A Comprehensive View of the Catholic
Sacrament of Reconciliation*

There are Catholics who see the sacrament of reconciliation merely as a means to cleanse themselves of sin in order to make heaven at the end of their lives. To see the sacrament of reconciliation in this way is to see it in an incomplete way, because heaven begins in this world. The perfection will only come at the end of time. Seeing the sacrament of reconciliation as having value only for the end of time, comes with the tendency of one living in sin, hoping Saturdays are days to clear off all of our sins. In a situation like this, there is bound to be the difficulty in seeing the relationship between the idea of reconciliation and Sunday to Saturday life. Every day of our lives should be in accordance with the will of God. A break from this, as mentioned, simply dumps us into a life that robs us of the heavenly situation and peace that God intends us to enjoy when He willed us into existence. The emphasis therefore should not be on the sacrament of reconciliation cleaning us for heaven alone, but also to get us back into the will of God in our daily living, where we can get the utmost and the greatest good from life.

The main idea that has been running through this discourse only reminds us once again the aim of Christ when he said that *he came that we may have life and have it abundantly (Jn. 10:10)*. In other words, He has come not to detract from our lives but to make our lives even more. This whole idea is also supported when God speaking in the prophecy of Jeremiah says: *my plan for you is that of welfare and not evil, to give you a future and a hope. (Jeremiah 29:11-14)*. No wonder the Catholic Catechism reiterating all of these emphasizes that the human person is made by God to share in the *blessed life of God (Catholic Catechism: Prologue. Par.1)*.The blessed life of God as indicated here has limitless joy for the human person.

The idea of penance or satisfaction still remains to be clarified. Usually in the confessions, the priest gives penance. It could be saying of some prayers or doing of some works. The observation is that some Catholics complain sometimes that the penance is too small. The fact is that the penance that is given is not meant to do something that amounts in the strict sense to make-up for the sin that one has committed. The God that we have offended by our sins is infinite. In the strict sense, if we are to do something that is to make up, it has to be infinite. But this is beyond the human person because he or she is finite. This is precisely the reason for the sacrifice of Christ on the cross. Christ is God, he is infinite and only His sacrifice could adequately make-up for our sins. The penance we are given by the priest therefore is in a sense to make us participate in the sacrifice of Christ. It is also a sort of practical way showing our remorse for our sins and our desire to make amend for our sins even if we cannot make-up for them in the manner Christ did. In summary, the smallness of the penance we are given ultimately demonstrates the love of God for the human person and the readiness of God to reconcile himself to us without expecting anything from us except our readiness to be united to Him (God.) Penance or satisfaction therefore unites our spirits with the whole spirit of reconciliation, reconciliation with God.

Through the given penance, we display our inner readiness to be united to God, the source of our lives. Penance then could be considered as our little token to make up for our sins against God, the loving father. In the above light, please let us not be disappointed when we are given little penance. Human beings cannot do anything to adequately make-up for our sins against God, the infinite one.

CHAPTER FIVE

On Confessing to a Human Person

With reference to the priest, some people sometimes ask: why do Catholics confess to a human person like them? A question like this only needs the light of Catholic theology. In the first place, through the initiative of God who is the giver of all intelligence, Christ is the chief reconciler of the world to God. But while Christ was to leave the world and in accordance with the will of the father He handed His mission of reconciling the world to God to His apostles. He thus says, "As the father has sent me, so am I sending you". He breathed on them saying, "receive the Holy Spirit, whosoever sins you forgive they are forgiven and whosoever sins you retain, they are retained". (Jn. 20:21-23). The church founded by Christ and His apostles therefore continues the mission of Christ, that of reconciling the world to the father. The priest represents the church and forgives sins in the name of the church. Through the laying on of hands on him during his ordination, he is enabled to share in the ministry of the apostles and thus the ministry of Christ in the world. He therefore forgives sins, not through his own power, but through the power of God. Although he is required to be holy, his power to forgive sin is valid not because of his personal holiness but by the power of God that works through him. Only God knows why He makes the choice of each particular priest; even every priest also needs to be reconciled to the Father because he too sins and needs reconcili-ation to God. No wonder the book of Hebrew says:

For every high priest chosen from among men is appointed to act on behalf of men in relation to God, to offer gifts and sacrifices for sins. He can deal gently with the ignorant and wayward, since he, himself is beset with weakness. Because of this he is bound to offer sacrifice for his own sins as well as for those of the people. (Heb. 5: 1—3).

At this juncture, we must remember the writings of Father Oscar Lukefahr, where he reminds us of the thinking of psycholo-gists in relation to the person living in guilt. He expressed that psychologists think that when we keep guilt and other nega-tive feelings inside, they cause stress which is harmful to our emotional and physical healthy. According to him, psychologists point out that talking about our guilt with another person has a cleansing effect and helps us gain new insight to face the future. In addition, Father Lukefahr mentions that many prominent Prot-estants leaders now say that it is not enough to just "confess our sins to God". They point out the necessity of confessing our sins to another human being and that such "confessing" offer many spir-itual benefits (father Oscar Lukefahr 1993:91-93).

The testimonies of psychologists and the Protestant leaders as Father lukefahr expresses only point to the wonderful wisdom of God in initiating and establishing the Catholic sacrament of rec-onciliation. In the catholic sacrament of reconciliation, accord-ing to the design of God, we not only can talk to a human being about our guilt and other negative feelings, but we can also hear the voice of God through the Human being, the priest, forgiving us our sins, the cause of our guilt and other negative feelings and pray for our overall peace. This indeed is a very fantastic reality in our lives as human beings made by a creator who is good and lov-ing by nature.

The sacrament of reconciliation, it must be noted, adds to the life that we already have by removing all guilt and negative feelings; the sacrament is available to return our whole being to its original state. It is friendly, because it works for our well-being. It dishes out all evils out of our bodies to enable us feel the greatest peace possible; it assists to keep our focus on our mission on earth, that is, having a wonderful life by living in accordance with the will of the giver of life, God (John 10:10). Indeed, the sacrament of reconciliation is an act of God to get the human person into the state that will enable him or her to get the utmost from life.

REFERENCES

Cathechism of the Catholic Church
        Second edition, revised in accordance with the official Latin text promulgated by Pope John Paul 11 (Vatican: Liberia Editrice, 1994)

John Paul 11, <u>Rich in Mercy</u>
        Encyclical
        Dives in Misericordia
        Nov. 30, 1980

Lukefarh, Oscar (Father) C.M., <u>The Priviledge of Being Catholic</u>
        (USA: Liguori, 1993)

Merriam-Websters Collegiate Dictionary
        Tenth Edition
        USA: Merriam-Websters, 2000

The Documents of Vatican 11
        All sixteen official text promulgated by the ecumenical council 1963-1965
        Walter M. Abbot, S.J (General Editor)

The Holy Bible
        Revised Standard Version
        (New York: Penquin Group, 1962)

ACKNOWLEDGEMENT

If not for the goodness and mercy of God, this work would not have been possible. I am grateful to God for his special care over my life especially for the gift of my spiritual father, Most Rev. Dr. John Okeoghene Afareha, the Bishop of Warri Catholic Diocese, Warri. God, I am grateful for the gift of him. A lovely spiritual father!

My parents, Sir and Lady M.P. Ukutsemuya are beyond description with words! They gave birth and had so much love for the one given birth to. They were always there in good and bad times. I acclaim you as best parents. May God reward you abundantly for all sacrifices that you have made. In the same vein I greet my siblings and relatives for being so supportive in my responding to God`s invitation to spread the kingdom of God. God bless you!

Family members are important. However, their efforts will be in vain without the support of the good people we have in the world. I therefore remember all, especially friends and colleagues who have played various roles in assisting me to remain in the priesthood for these years doing my little bit in the furtherance of God`s will in the world. I wished I had done more! But I realize nothing happens without the knowledge of God. He is in charge of all!

Thank you Stanley Kueberuwa, Gray Kueberuwa, Chief Joel

Akporehe, Hon. Dennis Omovie and a host of other nice people.

Greetings to all my Rev Father brothers especially Very Rev Fr Dr Edwin Erimeyoma who did the first vetting of this work; Very Rev Fr Dr Abaka Oghenejode, a wonderful brother; Very Rev Fr Dr Peter Akpoghiran who generously shows the way; I greet colleagues at the Federal University of Petroleum Resources, Effurun; the members of St John`s Catholic Chaplaincy, FUPRE; the members of Holy Trinity Catholic Church, Ugbomro and all other parishes and places I worked before. If not for the limited space here, I would have mentioned you all. I am indeed grateful to you all.

Mr Emmanuel Esemedafe, thank you for proof reading this work. Thank you all so very much for your benevolence towards me. God bless!

Rev. Fr. Dr. Joachim Ireruke Ukutsemuya

(St Dominic Savio, Niger Cat, Ekpan/ Federal University of Petroleum Resources, Effurun)

ABOUT THE AUTHOR

Joachim Ireruke Ukutsemuya

Rev Fr Dr Joachim Ireruke Ukutsemuya has a B.A (Hons), M.A and Ph.D degrees in Philosophy from the renowned University of Ibadan, Ibadan, Nigeria and a Bachelor of Theology from Urban University of Rome. He taught Philosophy in the major seminary of Ss Peter and Paul, Bodija, Ibadan from 1999-2003 as a member of the formators' team.  He was once the Dean of Students' Affairs in the Federal University of Petroleum Resources, Effurun where as the current Director of the Directorate of General Studies he still continues to lecture Philosophy under the Directorate of General Studies since joining the University in 2008 as the pioneer lecturer and co-ordinator of the General Studies and Entrepreneurial skills Unit that developed into a Directorate.

Dr Joachim Ukutsemuya has published several scholarly papers in local and international revered journals in his field. He has flare for issues of approach to life (culture), the human person and development. He intellectually explores all ways to ensure the good life for the human person. The free, satisfactory and comfortable existence of the human person is a strong motivation for his intellectual exploits.

He intellectualizes, Philosophizes and theologizes to ensure a better world and existence, that is, the good life for humans.